The Lottery Rose

Irene Hunt

TEACHER GUIDE

NOTE:

The trade book edition of the novel used to prepare this guide is found in the Novel Units catalog and on the Novel Units website. Using other editions may have varied page references.

Please note: We have assigned Interest Levels based on our knowledge of the themes and ideas of the books included in the Novel Units sets, however, please assess the appropriateness of this novel or trade book for the age level and maturity of your students prior to reading with them. You know your students best!

ISBN 978-1-56137-501-1

To order, contact your local school supply store, or:

Toll-Free Fax: 877.716.7272
Phone: 888.650.4224
3901 Union Blvd., Suite 155
St. Louis, MO 63115

sales@novelunits.com

novelunits.com

Table of Contents

Summary 3

Initiating Information and Activities...........................3

Fourteen Chapters 14
    Chapters contain: Vocabulary Words,
    Discussion Questions and Activities,
    Predictions, Supplementary Activities

Post-reading Questions 25

Vocabulary Activities...............................25

Glossary...27

Center Activities 28

Skills and Strategies

Thinking
    Brainstorming, comparing
    and contrasting, evaluating,
    analyzing details

Comprehension
    Predicting, sequencing,
    inference, problem solving
    and decision making

Literary Elements
    Character, setting, plot,
    theme

Writing
    Ads, directions

Vocabulary
    Antonyms/synonyms, words
    in context, base or root
    words

Listening/Speaking
    Participation in discussions,
    participation in dramatic
    activities, role play

Summary

Beaten and terrorized by his alcoholic mother and her boyfriend, seven-year-old Georgie is rescued by neighbors, taken to a hospital, and sent to a boys' home run by nuns. His prized possession is a rosebush which he has won in a lottery. Georgie insists on planting it in the garden across the street from the boys' home and when the owner of the garden, Mrs. Harper, angrily digs it up, Georgie hates her. Mrs. Harper has lost her husband and son who was Georgie's age. Her other son, Robin, is retarded, and becomes devoted to Georgie. Robin drowns and Georgie turns to Mrs. Harper and wants to be her son.

Notes: Please be selective, and use discretion when choosing the activities that you will do with the unit. It is not intended that everything be done, but that discretionary choices made are most appropriate for your use and group of students. A wide range has been provided, so that individuals as well as groups may benefit from these selections.

Initiating Activities

To the teacher: It is recommended that you acquire some background information pertaining to the policies regarding foster care and abused children in your area. (See pages 4-5 in this guide.) You may wish to make contact with someone in the legislative system willing to come in to the classroom to speak to your students, as well as a judge, reporter, social worker, foster parent, and a foster child. Try to provide as much accurate, current information to your students as possible.

Open the book, *The Lottery Rose*, and read the first paragraph of the story to the students in the group.

Use the brainstorming circle on the bulletin board, and define abused child. Find out just how much the students know about this topic. Have a discussion pertaining to foster care, and the reasons for placing children in this type of care. (See Glossary, page 27 for definitions.)

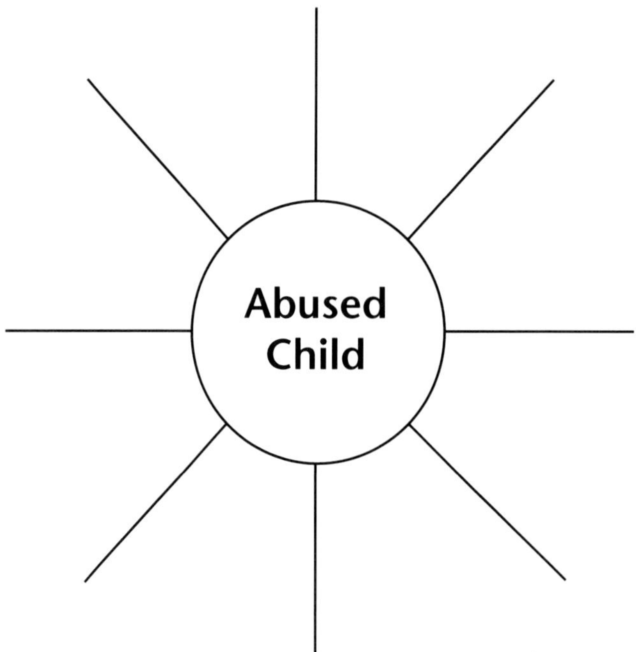

Some things to know about foster care

1. Children in foster care come from many places. They are from rich and poor neighborhoods from cities, small towns, and farm areas, and from families of every color and background.

2. Many children are in foster homes for a long time, and many families don't get help with their problems. Foster care is not supposed to be permanent. Judges in juvenile court, who put children in foster homes, should make sure that families get help with their problems. Social workers usually are the ones who help families with problems.

3. Children in foster care are supposed to be able to see their families. Sometimes that might not happen if a parent is very sick or in treatment.

4. If and when the family's troubles are solved, the child will go back to the family. A child is not kept in a foster home any longer than is absolutely necessary. This is the goal of everyone who helps. It is generally believed that long-term foster care creates identity and adjustment problems. If the troubles with the family can't be helped, then the child will not go back to his/her family.

5. Every child has the right for a chance to grow up in a loving family. When a judge decides that family troubles are too serious, and probably will not get better, then the child in foster care is given the chance to be adopted by a family that will love him or her. Decisions as to the placement ideally are made as soon as possible so that the child will know what is going to happen.

6. States have different names for the agency and division within that agency that are responsible for foster children. The name and number to call to contact the particular agency can be found in the telephone book under the name of the state.

7. Anyone interested in being a foster parent may call the same agency and ask for information. All adults, whether married or single, can apply. They must fill out applications, provide character references, and have several interviews with social workers to make sure that they are good people before they are approved as foster parents. Then they are given training in being a good foster parent.

Bulletin Board Idea

Cover the bulletin board with plain background paper. On it put a large brainstorming circle, with the words "foster home" in the center.

Previewing the Book

Look at the front and back cover of the book. What do you think the boy is thinking? Who is the woman in the background? What makes you curious about the story as you read the back cover?

Recommended Procedure

This book may be used in several ways: a) read to the entire class; b) read with the class; c) read in reading groups; d) read by an individual.

This book may be read one chapter at a time using the DRTA, Directed Reading Thinking Activity, Method. This technique involves reading a section, and then predicting what will happen next by making good guesses based on what has already occurred in the story. The predictions are recorded, and verified after the subsequent reading has taken place. (See pages 8-9 of this guide.)

The Discussion Questions and Activities at the end of each chapter, as well as any Supplementary Activities are provided so that you may, using discretion, make selections from them that will be suitable for use by the children in your group.

You may wish to have students show knowledge of words in the vocabulary before reading the chapter by writing simple definitions in their own words. After reading, the students may need to redefine the words by referring to the text and/or a dictionary.

Anticipation Guide

Directions: Attitudes may be changed by a book. To test that idea, read each of these statements. Put a check if you agree before reading. Save the sheet and look at the statements after reading. Were there any differences? Why? Explain in a sentence or two.

	Before reading	After reading
1. There's no use in feeling sorry for yourself.	__________	__________
2. If your parents do something to make you angry, you should talk to them about it.	__________	__________
3. Sometimes life is so hard it would be better not to go on living.	__________	__________
4. Boys shouldn't cry.	__________	__________
5. Hiding your feelings is good.	__________	__________
6. Some parents are incapable of caring for and supporting their children.	__________	__________
7. To keep on top of things, stay positive.	__________	__________

Graphic Organizers

Included in the Novel Unit are several types of graphic organizers, such as the Venn diagram, the T-Diagram, and brainstorming or cluster circles. A variety of possible answers should be listed by the teacher either on large sheets of paper or the chalk board. Only then should the students be asked to develop their own graphics. Students are encouraged to express their opinions, and to state what they know about a topic. The teacher lists these opinions and "facts" and later, as the children read and discover that some of their ideas are incorrect, these ideas may be crossed out on the sheets or board. Students should be encouraged to elaborate on their answers, justify their opinions, prove their predictions, and relate what they have read to their own lives.

T-Diagrams show likenesses and differences of two characters, plots, settings, etc.

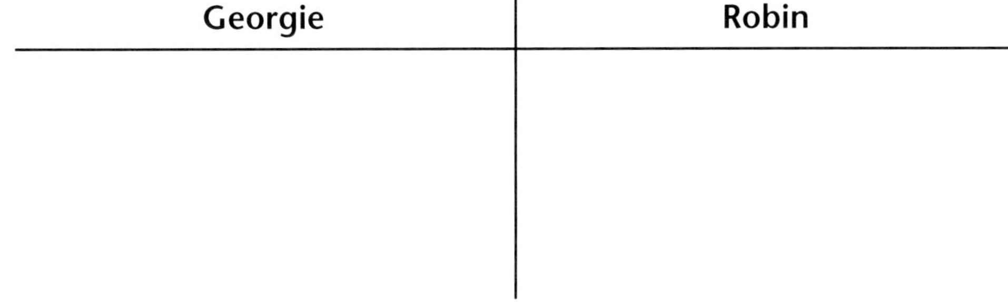

Venn diagrams are taken from math. Characteristics of two characters are listed, and the overlap or similarity may be seen.

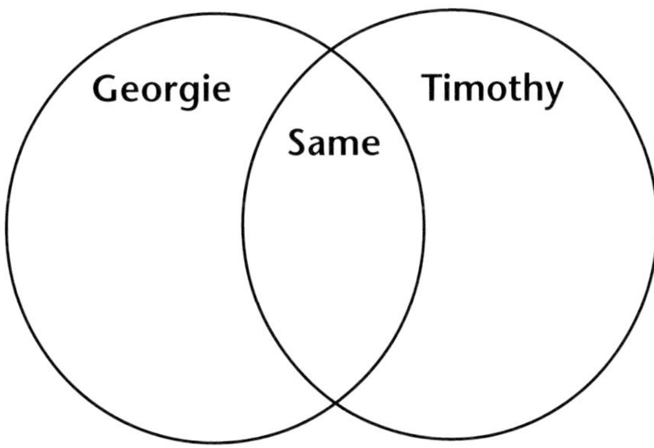

7

Using Predictions

We all make predictions as we read—little guesses about what will happen next, how a conflict will be resolved, which details will be important to the plot, which details will help fill in our sense of a character. Students should be encouraged to predict, to make sensible guesses as they read the novel.

As students work on their predictions, these discussion questions can be used to guide them: What are some of the ways to predict? What is the process of a sophisticated reader's thinking and predicting? What clues does an author give to help us make predictions? Why are some predictions more likely to be accurate than others?

Create a chart for recording predictions. This could be either an individual or class activity. As each subsequent chapter is discussed, students can review and correct their previous predictions about plot and characters as necessary.

Use the facts and ideas the author gives.

Use your own prior knowledge.

Apply any new information (i.e., from class discussion) that may cause you to change your mind.

Predictions

8

Prediction Chart

What characters have we met so far?	What is the conflict in the story?	What are your predictions?	Why did you make those predictions?

Using Character Webs

Attribute webs are simply a visual representation of a character from the novel. They provide a systematic way for students to organize and recap the information they have about a particular character. Attribute webs may be used after reading the novel to recapitulate information about a particular character, or completed gradually as information unfolds. They may be completed individually or as a group project.

One type of character attribute web uses these divisions:

- How a character acts and feels. (How does the character act? How do you think the character feels? How would you feel if this happened to you?)

- How a character looks. (Close your eyes and picture the character. Describe him/her to me.)

- Where a character lives. (Where and when does the character live?)

- How others feel about the character. (How does another specific character feel about our character?)

In group discussion about the characters described in student attribute webs, the teacher can ask for backup proof from the novel. Inferential thinking can be included in the discussion.

Attribute webs need not be confined to characters. They may also be used to organize information about a concept, object, or place.

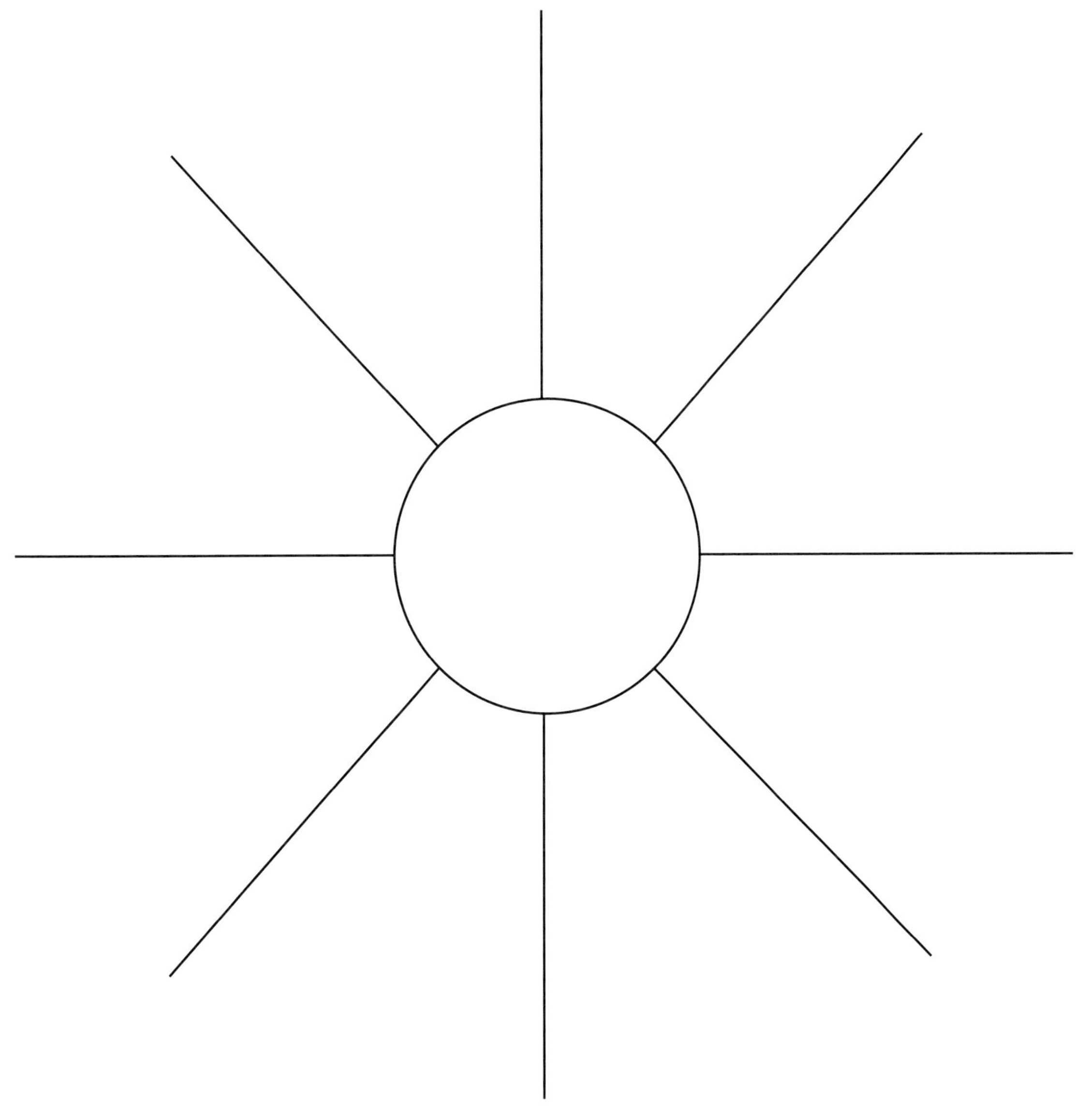

The attribute web below will help you gather clues the author provides about a character in the novel. Fill in the blanks with words and phrases which tell how the character acts and looks, as well as what the character says and what others say about him or her.

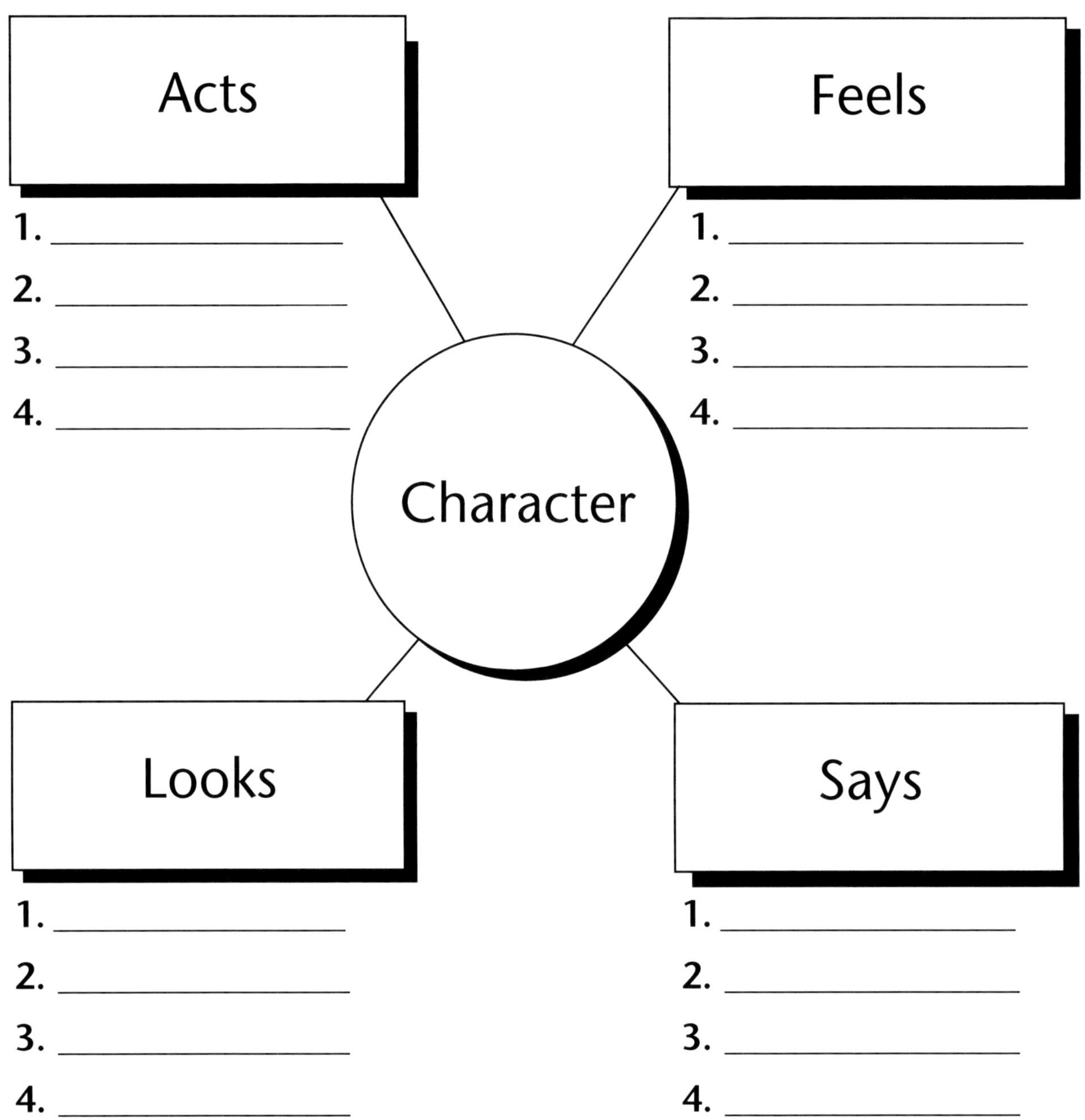

Story Map

Setting

Problem

Goal

Episodes

Resolution

Characters____

____

Time and Place____

____

Problem____

____

____

Goal____

____

____

Beginning ———→ Development ———→ Outcome

____

____

____

____

Resolution____

____

____

____

Chapter One—Pages 1-18

Vocabulary

welts 6	battered 7	wishfulness 8	intermission 11
impudent 11	wary 11	stealthily 12	vile 12
brute 13	scuttled 15		

Discussion Questions and Activities

1. Why do you think Georgie had not learned to read? *(pages 1-3)*

2. What do we know about Georgie? Begin an attribute web for him. (See pages 10-12 of this guide.)

3. Compare Ellen Ames to Miss Cressman using a T-Diagram.

Ellen Ames	Miss Cressman
librarian	teacher
thoughtful	cross

4. Georgie was not a perfect boy. What wrong things did he do? *(Page 3, He set a fire under a car, played hooky, and lied.)*

5. Why was Georgie hesitant to say he liked flowers? *(pages 4-5)* Do you think liking flowers is sissy-like? Why or why not?

6. How could Miss Cressman have handled the class's giggles? *(page 5)* Why didn't she like Georgie? *(Page 17, He set a fire under her car; he smelled because he didn't take baths and his mother didn't wash his clothes.)*

7. Why was Georgie afraid of his mother and Steve? *(Page 6, They drank, beat him, and did not treat him as a child should be treated.)*

8. Why do you think Mrs. Sims and Ellen Ames were kind to such a dirty, homely little boy like Georgie?

Prediction

Will Georgie win the lottery? What could he win? Remember that this is a small store lottery.

Supplementary Activities

1. A story map is an outline that helps you to understand and remember the story better. What do you know about the story after reading only the first chapter?

   - What is the setting?
   - Who is the main character?
   - What is the problem?

   As the story is read, more characters may be added and the setting and the problem may change, so additions may be made. Fill in the story map on page 13.

2. Dual-Entry Literature Log: Have students keep a separate, spiral-bound notebook in which they react to each section of the story that they have read and/or make predictions about what will happen. Tell students that they are to briefly summarize the story in the left-hand column, and to give their thoughts and feelings about it in the right-hand column. The teacher, in turn, writes entries—or separate letters—in response to the ideas in the student entries.

   Sample student reactions might begin: This makes me think of the time—If I were (character's name) I would…

   Notes—   Comments—

3. Chapter Titles: This novel does not have chapter titles. A writer usually uses chapter titles to indicate something that might happen or to create suspense to encourage the reader. After you read a chapter, write what you think would be the best chapter title. The teacher will post all titles and the class will vote for the best. The best chapter titles will be listed on the bulletin board.

Chapter Two—Pages 19-32

Vocabulary

flogged 22	irks 22	sheepishly 25	frenzy 26
decrepit 26	taunting 30	palmetto 30	

Discussion Questions and Activities

1. Why did Georgie worry about Steve destroying whatever he might win? *(Page 21, Steve had killed his kitten, and taken the colored pencils.)*

2. Why did Georgie's mother put up with Steve? *(Page 23, "If we don't have Steve, we ain't going to eat…")*

3. Would any of the other prizes have made Georgie happy? *(page 25)* Why do you think the rosebush was so special?

4. Why did Georgie have problems trying to find a place to plant the bush? *(Page 29, He wanted a place Steve and his mother would never see.)*

5. How could Georgie have avoided making Steve mad? *(Page 32, He should not have screamed.)*

Prediction
What could happen to Georgie?

Supplementary Activity
Research roses—their care—and the many varieties.

Chapter Three—Pages 33-51

Vocabulary
lurked 33	spasm 37	sponsor 41	bewilderment 42
monstrosity 43	pellet 48		

Discussion Questions and Activities
1. How and why was Georgie taken away from his mother? *(Pages 34 and 40, The police talked to Georgie and to the adults in the building and neighborhood. Georgie's mother and her boyfriend had repeatedly beaten and mistreated him according to witnesses.)*

2. How was the rosebush rescued? *(Page 36, The policeman asked the janitor to show him where he dumped it. The policeman found it and brought it back.)*

3. Why was Georgie placed in a special school? *(The judge decided that Georgie needed the special attention of the school.)*

4. Why couldn't Georgie have stayed with the Sims? *(Pages 38-39, There was no one to stay with him while the Sims worked. The Sims did not have much money and they were not young enough to take on the responsibility of a young child.)* Do you think a family or an institution will be the best place for Georgie?

5. How did Mrs. Sims show she really cared about Georgie? *(Page 43, She went along with the social worker to see where Georgie would live and go to school.)*

6. Georgie liked the flower beds across the street. What did he learn about the Harper family? *(Page 47, The little boy and father were killed. There is a retarded child, a sad mother and a grandfather living in the house across the street.)*

7. Why did Sister Mary Angela say that the rosebush could not be planted in Mrs. Harper's garden? *(Page 50, "Now that her husband is dead it [the garden] reminds her of him. She would never allow us to plant a strange flower or bush in her garden.")* If you were Sister Mary Angela, how would you handle Georgie?

8. What can we add to Georgie's character web?

9. Why do you think kids picked on someone like Georgie? How could Georgie have stopped this? *(page 48)*

Prediction

What will happen to the rosebush?

Supplementary Activities

1. Art: Have students create a bulletin board display depicting the characters they meet in the book, complete with the clothing or props which identify each. Draw and label the characters.

2. Make a large character chart. Add characters as we meet them in the novel. For each of the characters describe when they experienced the feelings listed. Add other characters and feelings if needed.

Feeling	Georgie	Timothy	Sister Mary Angela	Mrs. Harper	
Frustration					
Fear					
Pain					
Anger					
Relief					
Happiness					
Pride					
Grief					

Chapter Four—Pages 52-65

Vocabulary

sly 52	shrugged 60	anguish 61	encountered 62
stolidly 62	unyielding 62	cautiously 64	spasm 64
reassured 64	cowered 65		

Discussion Questions and Activities

1. Where did Sister Mary Angela suggest that Georgie plant his bush? *(the entrance of the building, a big flower garden, right outside his bedroom window, beside the statue on the lawn)* Why didn't Georgie accept any of the ideas? *(Page 53, Georgie had his mind set on the garden across the street.)*

2. What did Georgie learn from Mr. Collier? What kind of person was he? Is he like your grandfather? Compare using a T-Diagram.

Mr. Collier	My Grandfather
Pleasant voice	
Slender, old man	
Silver gray hair and beard	
Kind to grandson	

3. Georgie yelled out at Mr. Collier. Why do you think he did this? Did yelling help get the rosebush planted? *(pages 59-60)* What can you add to Georgie's attribute web?

4. How did Timothy and Sister Mary Angela treat the strange-acting Georgie? *(pages 60-62)* Do you think most boys at the home had problems adjusting?

5. Do you think that the bush will grow planting it without a spade or water? (page 65)

Supplementary Activity

Role Play/Interview: A panel of five students sits facing the class, which has prepared a list of questions to ask the characters in the story. Each panel member wears something and/or carries a simple prop which characterizes the role that person is assuming.

Chapter Five—Pages 66-70

Vocabulary

wretchedly 66　　　forlorn 67　　　strode 67　　　remorsefully 67
incinerator 68　　　imposed 69　　　mutilated 69

Discussion Questions and Activities

1. Why was Mrs. Harper so angry about Georgie planting the rosebush in her garden? Was she unreasonable? Was Georgie unreasonable? *(Pages 66-67, Both Georgie and Mrs. Harper could be said to be unreasonable but Georgie was definitely in the wrong by ruining the flowers at the Harpers'.)*

2. What was Mrs. Harper's terrible threat? *(Page 68, If she found the bush in her garden again, she would throw it in the incinerator.)*

3. How did Georgie react to Mrs. Harper's threat? Was this reasonable? *(Page 68, "...I'll set fire to your house—I'll kill you dead. I'll do the meanest things to you that ever happened...")* Does talk like this by children have much of an effect on adults?

4. What shocked Mrs. Harper? *(Page 69, She saw Georgie's back.)*

Prediction

What could happen to Georgie and the bush?

Supplementary Activities

1. Role play your way of handling a child like Georgie.

2. Draw a picture of Mrs. Harper and Georgie.

Chapter Six—Pages 71-81

Vocabulary

delirium 71　　　resultant 71　　　subsided 72　　　agitated 74
attuned 77　　　fret 80

Discussion Questions and Activities

1. What caused Georgie's illness and delirium? *(page 71, the beating, the sores that had not healed, a fever, the stress, and not eating)*

2. Why did Georgie think Sister Mary Angela was lying? *(Page 73, The story was too good to be real. Georgie thought of some of his mother's untrue stories.)*

3. How do you think Sister Mary Angela gained Georgie's confidence? *(page 74)* Why didn't Georgie think that Sister Mary Angela was lying now?

4. What do you think Georgie knew about God? What did Georgie say he'd ask God for? *(Page 77, "Have a policeman kill Steve and Miss Cressman—and her [Mrs. Harper].")*

5. What do you think Sister Mary Angela meant when she said, "I think we are not yet attuned to Thy Presence"? *(Page 77, She thought Georgie did not understand much about God and that we don't ask God to kill off people.)*

Prediction

What could happen to a hard-to-manage boy like Georgie? Will he make friends and fit into this school with his attitudes?

Chapter Seven—Pages 82-100

Vocabulary

glowering 83	sensitive 84	sullen 87	subdued 89
inattentive 89	destructive 89	incorrigible 89	congregating 92
envious 92	incinerator 99	foraging 100	vicious 100
strident 100			

Discussion Questions and Activities

1. How did Georgie respond to Mr. Collier's story reading? *(Page 83, Some parts of the story brought tears to Georgie's eyes; he put an arm around Robin.)*

2. Do you think Georgie believed what Mr. Collier said about his healthy rosebush? *(page 84)* Why or why not?

3. Why wouldn't Georgie keep the book? *(Page 86, It belonged to Mrs. Harper.)* What can we add to Georgie's character web?

4. How do you think Georgie learned to read so quickly? *(page 86)*

5. Why did Georgie like the story about the rosebush? *(Page 87, He helped write it.)*

6. Why do you think Georgie thought he was dumb? *(pages 86, 99)* Was Mr. Collier a good teacher? Why hadn't Georgie learned at his old school? *(Pages 89-90, He had been half-starved, beaten, and not helped by the teachers.)*

7. How did the boys help Georgie by inviting him to the sleep-out? Why was this unusual for Georgie? *(Page 93, "It was the first time Georgie could remember that another child had invited him to share something that promised to be fun.")*

Prediction

How will Sister Mary Angela and Mrs. Harper react to Georgie's early morning visit to the rose bush?

Chapter Eight—Pages 101-107

Discussion Questions and Activities

1. Why did Paul have to be very careful with Robin? *(Pages 101-103, Robin was retarded.)* What does the word retarded mean? Brainstorm.

2. Why do you think Robin liked Georgie? *(Page 105, The boy reminded him of Paul and good times with Paul.)*

3. What do you think Robin saw in the garden? Who was the lady helping the boy? *(page 106, Sister Mary Angela with Georgie)*

4. Why was it important and dangerous that Robin had found a way to get out of his bed? *(pages 105-106)*

Prediction

What clues do we have about what could happen in the story?

Chapter Nine—Pages 108-122

Vocabulary

discolorations 108	wary 113	incoherent 115	contentment 116
combatants 117	frostily 119	mutilated 120	defied 120
brusquely 122			

Discussion Questions and Activities

1. How had Georgie changed? *(Pages 109-110, He looked healthier, cleaner. He was learning to read.)*

2. What bad character trait did Georgie still have? *(Page 111, He was stubborn; he would not forgive Mrs. Harper.)*

3. Who paid Georgie's tuition at the school? *(page 111, Mrs. Harper)* Why do you think she did this?

4. To what did Sister Mary Angela compare Georgie's stubborn unforgiveness? *(pages 111-112, being stuck on snow and ice)*

5. Why did Georgie fight Richie? *(Page 117, Richie wanted Georgie to take off his shirt while he was swimming.)* Why didn't Georgie want to take off his shirt? *(His back was scarred from beatings.)* How do you think Georgie could have handled Richie without a fight?

6. Why do you think Georgie told Timothy the truth about his back? *(page 120)*

7. What is a friend? Brainstorm. How had Timothy shown that he was Georgie's friend?

Chapter Ten—Pages 123-135

Vocabulary

corralled 124	insolence 125	reproached 125	meditated 126
assure 129	persuaded 129	niche 129	boisterous 130
strides 131	grimacing 132	doted 134	majestically 134

Discussion Questions and Activities

1. How did Georgie begin helping Old Eddie in the garden? *(Page 123, Mr. Collier thought it would be good for Georgie to learn more about taking care of flowers since he liked them so much.)*

2. Why did Georgie want to believe that Mrs. Harper was not really Robin's mother? *(Pages 127-128, He made up a story about Mrs. Harper stealing Robin as a baby and putting a curse on him so he would not learn to talk or read. Georgie did not have happy memories about his mother and he had mixed up feelings about mothers. He did not know how mothers were to think, feel and act.)*

3. What kind of mistakes did Mrs. Harper make that Georgie caught? *(Pages 125-126, She left her pruning shears in the grass, and garden tools were left overnight in the wet grass.)*

4. What kind of a teacher was Georgie? How do you think he got Robin to say more words? *(pages 130-131)*

5. What did Georgie learn from Old Eddie about Mrs. Harper? *(Page 133-135, Mrs. Harper had had too much grief in her life. She loved both of her sons but in different ways.)*

6. What do you think Georgie was trying to say to his rosebush, "We've got to be good to each other, the way we always was before. Maybe some day—I thought when Old Eddie talked about her, that maybe some day—"? *(page 135)* How would you finish Georgie's sentence?

Chapter Eleven—Pages 136-148

Vocabulary

orchardist 137	treble 138	chorale 140	intermittently 140
ventured 144	versions 146	ominous 147	

Discussion Questions and Activities

1. What new talents or characteristics can we add to Georgie's attribute web? *(He was patient with Robin, a good gardener, and had a nice singing voice.)*

2. Why do you think Mrs. Harper decided to listen to the boys sing and then later to work with them on plays? *(Page 146, She hoped that working with boys who were Paul's age might help her.)*

3. What are some signs that Georgie might begin to change his feelings about Mrs. Harper? *(Page 147, "I wish I didn't have to keep her for my enemy—"; Page 148, Georgie talked to his rosebush about the play, "Never, —never—never—")*

Prediction
How will Georgie get around to making a friend of Mrs. Harper?

Chapter Twelve—Pages 149-166

Vocabulary

facial 149	enunciated 149	seclusion 149	complacently 151
scheming 152	sullenness 152	callous 156	grousing 156
forlornly 157	persistent 159	clamor 162	pompous 163
impudent 163			

Discussion Questions and Activities

1. Why do you think Georgie went to the play practices? *(Page 149, He was fascinated and he listened to the lines, learned the parts, and practiced with Robin as his audience.)* How did Mr. Collier learn that Georgie was an actor? *(Page 152, He found Georgie entertaining Robin with parts of the plays.)*

2. What unfortunate incident made it possible for Georgie to shine as an actor? *(Page 156, Kevin and Richie had a fight and Mrs. Harper put them out of the play.)*

3. Who helped Georgie to swallow his pride and get in on the play? *(page 159, Sister Mary Angela; page 160, Mr. Collier)*

4. What did Georgie's statement mean, "I wish we had words for an hour longer"? *(page 164)* What did Mrs. Harper mean by, "Grease paint gets into one's blood, Georgie"? *(page 164)*

5. After the play Georgie went out to his rosebush for a talk. What did he say? *(Page 165, "I talked to her [Mrs. Harper]...I liked her tonight...I wished she was my mother same as she is to Robin and to the boy that died—")*

6. What did Georgie plan to tell Mrs. Harper the next day? *(Page 166, "He wanted to go out and speak to her—to ask if she liked his acting, to tell her that she'd been a real good Alice and that her hair was prettier than any he had ever seen. He wanted terribly to hear the good things she might have to say to him...")*

Supplementary Activity
Role play Mr. Collier asking Georgie to take part in the play.

Chapter Thirteen—Pages 167-175

Vocabulary

garbled 170   scuttled 171   retrieving 171   chortled 175
relentlessly 175

Discussion Questions and Activities

1. Do you think it was Amanda's fault that Robin got away? *(page 171)* Robin heard the calls when he was down by the ducks. Why do you think he didn't answer?

2. How did Robin find a way out of the garden? *(Page 172, He watched a squirrel dart through a narrow opening between two bushes.)*

3. How did the ducks really cause the accident? *(Page 175, The ducks crowded around Robin making lots of noise and pecking at the bread in his hand. This frightened Robin and he tried to run away.)*

Prediction

What will happen to Robin?

Supplementary Activity

With cooperative groups, divide a sheet of drawing paper into four sections. What are the main parts of the story in this chapter? Class members may disagree. Illustrate the most important parts of this chapter. Add thought balloons for the most important speeches.

Chapter Fourteen—Pages 176-185

Vocabulary

preceding 176   rites 176   accompaniment 177   haggard 178
clamoring 183

Discussion Questions and Activities

1. How did Georgie help or participate in Robin's funeral? *(Page 178, He sang with the boys.)*

2. Why did Georgie dig up his rosebush? *(Page 182, Georgie did not want to leave Robin out in the cemetery by himself.)* Why didn't Georgie accept Mrs. Harper's offer to buy another rosebush? *(Page 182, "This is the only rosebush that Robin would love—it's the only one that's right for him. He has to have this one.")*

3. Georgie asked Mrs. Harper if he had been "born" to her. How did Mrs. Harper answer? *(Page 184, "I didn't 'born' you, but you're mine—no matter where I go or what I do—")* Why do you think she said that?

4. What do you think will happen to Georgie and Mrs. Harper?

Post-reading Questions

1. Setting: Could we have had the story of *The Lottery Rose* with a different setting? Why or why not?

2. Theme: What was the author's message? Why do you think the author wrote this story? What do you think is the most important thing to remember about this story?

3. What is a hero? Is Georgie a hero? Why or why not?

4. Complete the story map. How many episodes were there? What was the problem of the story and how was it resolved?

5. Plot: Choose three events in the story, and write two or three paragraphs about how changing these events would have changed what happened in the story. For example, how might the story have been different if the Sims had kept Georgie?

6. Character: Look at Georgie's character web. Has Georgie changed? Should we remove some of the attributes?

7. Choose your favorite scene to dramatize.

Vocabulary Activities

1. Draw pictures to remember the definitions.

2. Play charades to dramatize words.

3. Place the words for the day in categories:

Things	Descriptive	Actions	Feelings	Pioneer Language

Categories may be added as new words in the unit are introduced. The words and categories may be placed on a Word Wall.

4. Students may pick two words from the displayed lists and tell how they might be related.

5. Words in Context: Ask students to "guess" at the meaning from context, telling why for each guess. Make a list of "why answers" to teach context clues.

6. List the vocabulary words for the day on the board or on a sheet of paper in the form of a table. Pronounce the words. Ask the students to rate their knowledge of each of the words as a group or individually.

Word	I Can Define	I Have Heard	I Don't Know

7. Find the base or root word for each vocabulary word. What prefixes or suffixes were added? What is the meaning of the root word? How did the prefix or suffix change it?

8. Put the vocabulary words for the day into sets of two words each. Use each set of words in a sentence. Choose one sentence to illustrate.

9. Read the sentence in which each of the vocabulary words is used. Write your own definition of each word. Check your definition with that given in the dictionary.

10. Students will make predictions about how the author will use the vocabulary: setting, characters, problem, action.

11. The students will develop word maps. They will use color to distinguish antonyms, synonyms, etc. This activity may be done in cooperative groups.

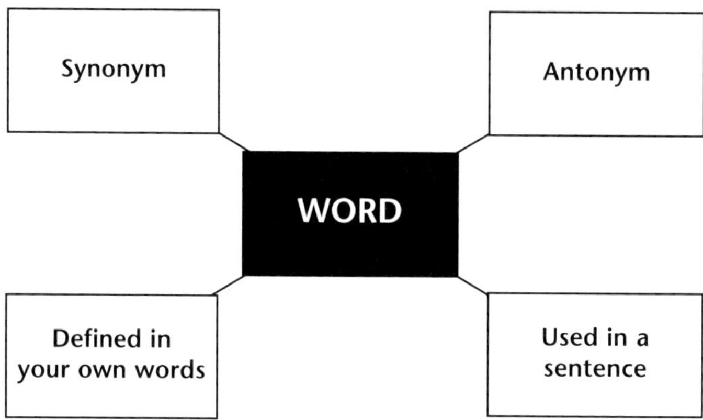

12. Take the vocabulary words for several chapters. Play a 20 questions-type game (pairs, groups, or whole class). One student, or the teacher, selects a word for the class or group to identify by asking up to 20 questions (or 10 questions) about that word which may be answered by "yes," "no" or "sometimes."

13. For each of the vocabulary words write a sentence that makes sense. Omit the vocabulary word. Make an answer key on the back of the paper. Share your sentences with a classmate.

14. Each student or cooperative group will make a poster, banner, or sign to advertise their word or words. The ad must show what the word means and how to pronounce it. The words will be displayed and should be signed by the artist(s).

15. Use a "Trivial Pursuit" board with vocabulary words and definitions on 3x5 cards for each category. Players must give the word for the definition which is read aloud to score.

26

Glossary

Adopt: To take someone else's child as a member of your family. Adopted children stay with their new family until they are grown, for people adopt a child because they really want to have a child and are willing to be responsible for taking care of that child.

Affection: Loving feelings shown by words and actions.

Attention: Noticing a child and what that child is needing.

Court: A meeting with a judge (and sometimes a jury) where the judge decides if someone has broken the law or if someone with serious problems should get help for those problems.

Foster Care: Care given to a child whose own family can't or doesn't give that child what he or she needs to grow up healthy and whole.

Foster Home: A place where a child lives with a family not related to him or her for a while. Here the child is cared for by that family as if they were his or her family. The child does not usually stay with this family until he or she is grown. A foster family often has more than one foster child at one time.

Judge: The person in charge of the court who sees that the rules of the court are obeyed, and who decides if someone has broken the law or if someone needs help for very serious problems.

Juvenile Court: A special court for children under 18 years old (juveniles) who need help or who have broken the law.

Physical Abuse: When one person hurts another person which leaves marks, and it isn't an accident.

Social Worker: A person whose job is to help people with serious problems. Social workers also make sure that children are well cared for. They help to find foster or adoptive parents when the biological parents cannot take care of their child.

Center Activities

Create a flower garden. Have several garden catalogs available in the area. Make a grassy scene on the bulletin board. Tell the children to "plant" a flower in the grass. Choose one of the following activities:

1. **Sponge Paint**—To create a flower you will need the following materials:

   Paper (any kind)   Sponges, cut to desired size/shape
   Thick tempera paint   Pie tins or shallow dishes, for paint

   a)   Pour the paint into the pie tin or dish.
   b)   Dip the surface of the sponge into the paint, running the sponge along the edge of the paint container, to remove the excess paint.
   c)   Dab the sponge onto the paper to get the desired effect.
   d)   Use different sponges for different colors of paint.
   e)   Allow to dry on a flat surface.

2. **Dyed Flowers**—To create dyed flowers you will need:

   Newspapers   Paint shirts
   Round coffee filters   Food coloring
   Containers, such as margarine tubs for the coloring

   a)   Put the newspapers down on a flat surface.
   b)   Mix some food coloring into water in the containers. Have the children wear paint shirts when doing this activity.
   c)   Fold a coffee filter repeatedly until it resembles a small cone.
   d)   Quickly dip the filter into a color of choice and repeat. The color will then spread over a portion of the filter.
   e)   Turn the filter and repeat the procedure on its side, and then on its top.
   f)   Carefully open the filter and place it on the newspapers to dry. This will be the "bloom" of the flower.
   g)   When the filter is dry, a stem and leaves may be made from the colored paper.